GHOST T

GHOST TRAIN

Sean O'Brien

Oxford   New York
OXFORD UNIVERSITY PRESS

Oxford University Press, Walton Street, Oxford OX2 6DP

Oxford New York
Athens Auckland Bangkok Bombay
Calcutta Cape Town Dar es Salaam Delhi
Florence Hong Kong Istanbul Karachi
Kuala Lumpur Madras Madrid Melbourne
Mexico City Nairobi Paris Singapore
Taipei Tokyo Toronto
and associated companies in
Berlin Ibadan

Oxford is a trade mark of Oxford University Press

First published in Oxford Poets
as an Oxford University Press paperback 1995

British Library Cataloguing in Publication Data
Data available

Library of Congress Cataloging in Publication Data
O'Brien, Sean, 1952–
Ghost train / Sean O'Brien.
p. cm.—(Oxford poets)
I. Title. II. Series.
PR6065.B744G46 1995 821'.914—dc20 95-9712
ISBN 0-19-283231-X

3 5 7 9 10 8 6 4 2

Printed in Hong Kong

For Rosa and Biddy Doonan,
and in memory of
Freda and David

ACKNOWLEDGEMENTS

Some of these poems have appeared or are due to appear in the following, to whose editors thanks are due: *Bête Noire*, *Braquemard*, *Gallimaufry*, *The Guardian*, *The Independent on Sunday*, *London Magazine*, *New Writing 4* (The British Council), *The Page* (The Northern Echo), *Pigeonhole*, *Poetry Review*, *The Rialto*, *Southern Review*, *The Times Literary Supplement* and *Verse*. Acknowledgements are also due to BBC Radio 3.

'Somebody Else' appeared in the anthology *The New Poetry*, edited by Michael Hulse, David Kennedy and David Morley (Bloodaxe, 1993). 'Special Train' appeared in the anthology *One for Jimmy*, edited by Matthew Sweeney (Hereford and Worcester County Council, 1992). 'Cantona' was commissioned by *On the Line* (BBC 2). 'The Commission' was commissioned by Tyne Tees Television. 'Poem Written on a Hoarding' was commissioned for the 1993 Hull Literature Festival. 'A Rarity' was published in an edition of fifty broadsheets by Carnivorous Arpeggio (!) Press (Hull) in 1993.

The author wishes to thank the Arts Council of Great Britain for a writer's bursary in 1992; Northern Arts and the Universities of Durham and Newcastle for the Northern Arts Literary Fellowship 1992–4; and the American Academy of Arts and Letters for the E. M. Forster Award in 1993.

CONTENTS

SOMEBODY ELSE

In fact you are secretly somebody else.
You live here on the city's edge
Among back lanes and stable-blocks
From which you glimpse the allegations
Of the gardening bourgeoisie that all is well.
And who's to argue? Lilac's beaten to the punch
By cherry blossom and the spire disappears
Among the leaves. Merely to think of
The ground-cover detail this outline implies,
The seeds and saplings and their names,
The little wayside trestles where they're bought,
The just-so cafés, the innumerable
And unnumbered high-hedged roads
For coming home down sleepily,
For instance—that would blind you
With a migraine, were one possible
In this redemptive climate. Sit.

It is somewhere you thought you had seen
From a train. You were not coming here.
It is something you thought was a striking vignette
By an as-yet-uncredited hand. It is somewhere
In moments of weakness at Worcester Shrub Hill
Or in Redditch or Selby you wished
You could enter. You already had. This is it,
The good place, unencumbered by meaning.
For hours no one comes or goes:
The birds, the light, the knowledge
That this place is endlessly repeated—
Is the known world and the elsewheres too—
Will do the living for you. Were you moved
To halve a gravestone you might find
That *England, 2pm* was written through it.

Long before now you've imagined
A woman at work in an attic,
Applying the back of her elegant wrist
To a strand of loose hair. She was sorting
A life, in a shaft of pale dust
Where a slate had come loose, but now

She is quite frankly reading. Kneeling
By a doll's house full of Guardsmen
She's stunned by what she thought she thought.
In the kitchen three storeys below
Are an unopened newspaper next to the hob
And a cat coming in, going out,
Like a trouper, addressing its bowl
In the permanent meantime through which
You come walking so fluently
People would think you belong.
As to the man in her life,
If you lived at a different hour
You'd see him performing his vanishing act
On the bridge by the station.
The train doesn't come, only noises.
A stiff breeze unsettles the fireweed,
Leading the eye to the drop where the stream,
Which is almost as real as the Boat Race,
Goes quietly down to the bend where it vanishes too.
As to sex, you have gained the impression
That somehow it's meant to encourage the others
Who might overrate or not do it at all,
Either way missing the point, although no one
As far as you know has yet clarified that.
The tree-shadows washing the ceiling,
The damp patch in bed, and her manner,
Both brisk and erotic, of pausing
To put up her hair before dressing,
All these suggest you are here.
What, then, of scholarship?
In the 'history room' whose fake stained glass
Is viewed with that tolerant humour
(What isn't?) are somebody's books
In a version of English you half understand.
You search the catalogue
Of the Festival of Britain
Repeatedly for evidence of you
And think it must have been mislaid.
When will you learn? What could it mean,
Conspiracy, when everyone conspires
Against themselves and does not know it?

REVENANTS

It's four o'clock, an autumn Sunday,
After a hailstorm and just before dark.
The dead are reassembling,
There beneath the dripping trees
Beside the pond, and more arrive
Continually by all the gates.
In the young middle-age of their times,
Demob suits and made-over dresses,
Men with their hands in their pockets
And women inspecting their patience
In compacts, they're waiting
As if there were something to add.

Friends, we are the unimagined
Facts of love and disappointment,
Walking among you with faces
You know you should recognize,
Haunting your deaths with the England
We speak for, which finds you
No home for the moment or ever.
You will know what we mean, as you meant
How you lived, your defeated majority
Handing us on to ourselves.
We are the masters now. The park's
A rainy country, ruining
The shoes you saved to wear to death,
In which we buried you.

INTERIOR

The fields and 'the wooded escarpments'
Inherit the shades of old furniture—
The dun and could-be-blood and lacks-conviction green
Of sofas jammed up rear passageways
In under-advertised hotels whose afterlife is spent
Not being read about in waiting-rooms.
The date is Nineteen Fifty-X. The residents
Have died but not been told. They jostle bonily
To hog the yellow *Telegraph* through days
In steep decline from gin-and-it
To after-dinner coma. Why detain them further?
As if there were choices, as if on the nod
You could crate them all up in the mind of God.
Deep in the retarded shires whose very
Names have been abolished, they persist,
Clandestinely, immortally defunct.
Now if we took that other turning
We should find them, arrayed in rank order
Across the parterre, stripped now
Of rivers and jungles, all rheumily glaring
As though the prow of our canoe displayed
A threatening announcement
They could very nearly read.
Though we go by a different route
We can smell the old country—a pillow
On a yellow face, the endless nagging corridors
Where damp and dust and gas contend.
It lingers in the senile tearooms
And in the crusty carpets of emporia
Where what's for sale is sentimental horror,
The used-to-be, the bad idea.
We hear the silence in the churches wait
For regiments disbanded on the Somme
To swim back through the mud and give
Due thanks, the ploughmen and the gentry
With their proper limbs restored.
Two Ridings later we come to the sea.
On this neglected coast it rolls
Indifferently ashore, a grey-white swell
Unburdening itself, then sliding back

4

Across the rotted boulder-clay
And muttering *history, history*, as if
That should explain these haunted roads,
Ancestral nowheres, *proper drains and class distinction.*

SPECIAL TRAIN

The service ran only on Sundays,
For free, from the sticks to the sticks
Along lines that were never discovered by Beeching.
From Coalville to Warsop, to Crowle and Dutch River,
The world was still driven by steam—
An apology, forty years late,
For a government exiled to history.
They smiled through the smoke from the pages
Austerity printed, believing it still.
No trouble was spared. Already delayed,
We would ride in authentic discomfort.
The carriages smelled of when everyone smoked.
In the corridors nurses and servicemen flirted,
Incurring the mass disapproval of character-actors
Distracted from *Penguin New Writing*.
The chill at the ankles, the seats unraised!
Soon we were somewhere in England,
Names all gone and shires camouflage,
A home from home in the indifferent
Grey-green that black-and-white made real,
Beneath a clear and silent sky which meant
That somewhere else would get it after dark.
We might think about this for a minute
While raising the eggs to our mouths.
I had my agenda. We all did.
I hoped I would finish up handcuffed
To Madeleine Carroll. Instead,
When I went the wrong way to the buffet
That never existed and found a compartment
So clearly forbidden I had to go in,
You were waiting and this was my fault.
We had to get on to the part where bad temper
Discloses a lifelong attachment
And do so without a hotel. We sat there
Not talking. Perhaps we could own it,
The glamorous boredom of evening.
The drunken stave of wires at the window
Played backwards as we watched a river
Swim its *s* away between the poplars
To the east, where glasshouse country

Flared against the dark. Now name that tune,
Sleep-music with its accents leaning north.
We might have lived like that,
Remote and unhistorical
Day-labourers for idle happiness.
You disagreed. Already, you told me,
Far off, at the unrationed end of the Fifties
A radio played a request to itself
In a room on the street we were born in—
Played at this hour on a similar Sunday—
And we were not listening. You studied your hair
In the darkening glass and I saw there
The matter-of-fact combination
Of scorn and indulgence I'd recognize later
As love. When you vanished you left me
A smoke-ring the shape of your kiss,
And the seats were all taken by sinister troupers
Denying in accentless English
Your very existence. No Madeleine either.
I thought it was love. It was politics,
Even on Sunday. Then when I woke up
We were braking to enter a county
Known neither to us nor the Ordnance Survey,
A theme park of oddments
Where tracks were converging
Past pill-boxes, scrubland and hawthorns,
Lamp-posts and slab-concrete roads,
To the ghost of a council estate
Where the fireweed brushed at the sills.
This part, we infer, was unwritten.
We've sat here at twenty past six
On the wrong side of England forever,
Like mad Mass Observers observing ourselves,
And if we should wonder what for, we must hope
That as usual it does not concern us.

THE POLITICS OF

When I walk by your house, I spit.
That's not true. I *intend* to.
When you're at breakfast with the *Daily Mail*
Remember me. I'm here about this time,
Disabled by restraint and staring.
But I do not send the bag of excrement,
Decapitate your dog at night,
Or press you to a glass of Paraquat,
Or hang you by your bollocks from a tree,
Still less conceal the small home-made device
Which blows your head off, do I, prat?
I think you'll have to grant me that,
Because I haven't. But I might.
If I were you, I'd be afraid of me.

April 1992

AUTUMN BEGINS AT ST JAMES'S PARK, NEWCASTLE

homage to James Wright

Under the arc, the Toon Army tsunami,
Under three o'clock's great cry on Gallowgate,
Remember the lost world, politics: cages flying
Up from the pit and disgorging their democrats,
Helmeted, in blackface, by the thousand,
Like the sappers of the Somme.

A seated army of convicts
Will be thundering WOR BALL
At faintheart southern referees all winter.

At freezing dusk the bloodbucket bars are stowed out.
Mortgaged to football, the underclass raises
A glass to the ghost of itself
In a world without women or work.

IN THE MIDST OF LIFE

All in the winter's afternoon
We walked by the canal—
My Victorian self and a certain girl
(My main squeeze and my pal).

Down through the drizzling early dusk
Our dialogue extended.
We lowered our spirits deep in the mud
Where our reflections ended.

That world was all that was the case,
Dead warehouses and water.
Having no option I walked on
With my lock-gate-keeper's daughter,

Past the fever hospital,
Past the lavish quicklime pit,
Past howling Bedlam and the gibbet
And all the rest of it,

Down to the basin where narrow-boats rot
While their colours leak into the reeds,
Where Tennyson meets the industrial might
Of Brummagem and Leeds.

She dangled her feet in the poison
And shook out her long black hair,
And taking my last piece of chewing gum
Said, 'Luvvy, it just isn't there.

Oh don't you ever get tired
Of merely perfecting the script?
It started to feel inauthentic
The last time my bodice was ripped.

The villain, I'd add, resembled yourself
With a dash of the owld Sean Bean,
But the act was like filling a form in
With a (perfectly civil) machine.'

''Tis strange,' I replied, 'for I cannot recall
That I've ever been wid yez till now,
And yet it says here we're supposed to engage
In a touch of the rowdy-ow-dow.'

'Well, we can't muck about with the lines,' she sighed,
Placing her gum on a brick.
'You show me yours and I'll show you mine.'
So we did the Wild Thing double quick.

After all, people are starving
For want of a gig and a wage.
You can't let your feelings prevent you
Performing what's down on the page.

You don't get a job in a theme park
And then keep your pants on as well.
You ought to be grateful you're lucky
And glad you've got arses to sell.

A RARITY

It's under the X where the viaducts met.
It was round the back and further down
And it isn't that street but a vanished
Identical elsewhere that waits
In a different night with a different accent
Beneath a blue sign reading TIXE.
Kelly's *Apocrypha* offers no entry
But don't let that stop you from wasting
The middling years in pursuit of a number
Whose title escapes you, a band you can't
Even remember or swear to have heard.
Polish your shoes, climb into bed
And breathe in the sweetness of nylon and Bass.
The girls are done up to the nines,
Like racoons with affective disorders,
Rehearsing three steps round their handbags
And speaking in smoke-rings, a code
Meaning *Fuck off and die* or *Be older*,
Knowing it's to you the management reserves
The right to do pre-emptive violence.
You almost believe in the night you went
In on a whim and came out on a stretcher
With VOX back-to-front on your forehead.
Rippling in its skin of sweat
The bar retires to infinity, bulb
After bulb swinging back to the stillness
Your dreaming's disrupted, the night
Before music and after, the night of un-music—
No horn-chart, no thin, underamplified Fender,
No workaday-beautiful backline, no voice
Being torn from the soles of the feet:
No such matrix, no such number.
Everything is afterwards, a dripping jacket
Hung across a mirror, drinks becoming syrup,
A van spitting teeth on its way to the knacker's.
The culture of almost is married, divorced
And has always been forty. Yet now you step in—
The wrong hole, the wrong wall, but at least
It's not there in the hours of business—
To run down a shuddering spiral that ends

In a foyer intriguingly minus a door.
Knee-deep in water and flyers, it smells
Like your big sister's hairspray, supposing
She'd used it or even existed.
Under the dandruff of whitewash and rust,
Behind traffic and ship-engines,
Wind in the stairwell, the pulse in your temple,
What you can hear will be nothing, the space
Made of wishing, the cousin of happiness,
Waiting to comfort the longing to know
There is something you still haven't got.
Why not pick up a leaflet? It mentions
The unnumbered white-label item
Unearthed by a rumour (one copy)
In Belgium. The price is an arm and a leg,
Your entire collection, your job and your marriage
And still you won't find it. It's perfect.

THE ALL–NIGHT AFTERNOON

Perhaps you are still awake now
In the midsummer half-dark beside me,
Hearing the sealed-in roar of trains
To whose drivers this night may be normal—
The moon on blue fields, the still sheep
Awaiting instructions, the sea over there
And the beams on the headlands revolving,
The ships on their fiery courses.

We ought to be starting a journey
Where nature and art have conspired
A result, but not even those passages
Closer to home have an interest in us—
Not the shush of laburnums and roses,
Not the silence that hangs between trains
After midnight, when summer comes up
For its long afternoon in the different language
We'd know, were we different too,
Having nothing but time on our hands.
The moon beats down. It is teaching us
Not to be here, and we cannot obey.

RAIN

At ten pm it starts. We can hear from the bar
As if somebody humourless fills in the dots,
All the dots on the window, the gaps in between.
It is raining. It rained and has always been raining.
If there were conditionals they too would rain.
The future tense is partly underwater. We must leave.
There's a road where the bus stop is too far away
In the dark between streetlights. The shelter's stove in
And a swill of old tickets awaits us.
Transitional, that's what we're saying,
But we're metaphysical animals:
We know a watery grave when we see it
And how the bald facts of brute nature
Are always entailed by mere human opinion,
So this is a metaphor. Someone's to blame
If your coat is dissolving, if rain is all round us
And feels like the threats-cum-advice of your family
Who know I am up and have come and will go to no good.
They cannot be tempted to alter their views
In the light of that sizzling bulb. There it goes.
Here we are: a black street without taxis or buses.
An ankle-high wave is advancing
To ruin your shoes and my temper. My darling,
I know you believe for the moment the rain is my doing.
Tonight we will lie in the dark with damp hair.
I too am looking for someone to blame. O send me
A metro inspector, a stony-faced barmaid.
The library is flooding and we have not read it,
The cellar is flooding and we shall be thirsty,
Trevor MacDonald has drowned as the studio shorts
And the weather-girl goes floating past
Like Esther Williams with her clothes on,
Mouthing the obvious: raining.
There's no need to labour the obvious, dearest, you say,
As you wring out your nylons and shoot me.

POEM WRITTEN ON A HOARDING

. . . Novembers, Decembers, you smoke-haunted Fifties: lead me
The wrong way to school, by the drain and the tenfoot,
The rain-rotted gate to the graveyard, the laurelled Victorian
Dark of the ruinous gardens, the fogged-over bombsites
Still pungent with bangers. Here's Josie-without-a-last-name,
The nuns and the dick-nurse. Diptheria. Football.
And here are the snow and that white, other city
I can't recall leaving, or ever re-enter.

ESSAY ON SNOW

We have been here before, but not often,
With the blue snow lying on the shaded roofs
And the city beyond them
Lying open, miles of it, with no one there—

Untrodden parks and freezing underpasses,
The statuary anonymous, the cobbled chares
Like streams of blackened ice.
There is a bird somewhere. Its voice

Is like chipping an icicle,
Damping the note, then trying again.
We have lived in the wrong place forever,
But now we can see what we meant,

The blue snow-shade behind the house,
The abandoned allotment, the shed,
The rags of willowherb, the one-note
Samba of the bird inside the ice.

HOUSE

From the bomb-damaged slates
To the submarine stink of the drains,
From the den in the tall, pithy elders
Up to the crook of the mulberry tree
With its view of the spare-bedroom mirror
From which we looked back at ourselves,
The house, my house, your house,
The general house of that time
And that class, in a district still dazed
And half-empty, arrested, it seemed,
At summer's end, got us by heart.
We wandered for years in its corridors,
Counting the footsteps from corner to corner,
Gazing up into the deadlight,
Inspecting the pictures of Bude and Amalfi
Where no one we knew ever went.
Parked on the stairs for an hour
Like victims of shock, we recited
Our tables, or *the Nidd the Ure the Aire*
The Wharfe the Calder and the Don.
We examined our Flags of the World.
We waited, and then as by magic
We turned up again and again at a door
Left ajar, at a room where one curtain
Was drawn on a chaos of papers
And upended drawers. On the desk
Was a bottle of ink which had set
Round the nib of a pen in mid-sentence,
A letter unwritten before we were born.
It was only the place and the date
In rusty italic. This got us nowhere,
But from it we learned that the question
Was not one of meaning but habit, a way
Of being there those off-white afternoons
When someone was always about to arrive
To claim the greatcoat flung across the chair
And fold the page and gently shoo us out
Before forgetting us entirely,
Going downstairs to start shouting
In Latinate paragraphs, hours on end,
About women and history, a problem
Whose cause, whose effect, we are pondering still.

OF ORIGINS

The middle-distant roar of trains
Maps in the miles of railway land,
The scrub-and-hawthorn nowhere-much
That murderers and children loved.

Garden of industrial remembrance
Plus an unexploded bomb, its obelisks
Were sheds and switching gear.
Its vast embankments aimed themselves

At absent bridges, cuttings ran
To seed among the dockleaves, and there too
Was always afternoon, a cold
And comforting evasion of the rules

With smut and cigarillos and your name,
Anne Broadwell, lavishly inscribed
In chalk on several hundred pipes
But rained away before you saw.

I sat inside the culvert's mouth
Past teatime, smoking, waiting for the snow
And reading *Penthouse*. I insist:
Et in Arcadia Ego.

LATINISTS

Trewartha, Gerald, Felix, Windy,
I see you ascending the stairs
From the Main Hall to heaven,
A place which I now understand
Is the school's upper floor, only bigger;
Ascending through clouds
In the era of pre-dustless chalk
To that rarefied zone
Where even *if* is absolute.
As the organist stumbles
Once more through the last verse
Of *Lord Receive Us With Thy Blessing*,
You go with the rags of your gowns still about you,
Stacks of North and Hillard in your arms,
Making for your far-off rooms
To wipe the board and start again
With the verb for *I carry*,
The noun meaning *table*.
I go to every room at once
And I still cannot listen,
Remember or scan, and the table's
Still strapped to my back.
When you ask me again what the subject might be
In this sentence, I still cannot answer—
O'Brien, it's not the full stop—
And still make the foolish suggestion
That sirs, in a sense, there is none,
Phenomenologically speaking, that is.
When the stare you award me
Takes longer than Rome did
To flower and vanish, I notice
The bells are not working in heaven today.

AWOL

The fat-fingered leaves of the chestnuts
Have lost their particular ochre.
Lying in swathes on the grass
They're reaching the unnoticeable stage
At the near edge of winter
When detail and distance are smudged.
Mourners and gravediggers stand for a moment
In yew-framed remoteness, appalled
And in love with the very idea of themselves.
Smoke travels sideways across the estates
As if this must still be the Fifties
And I have absconded. Omniscient nuns
And mad parkies are waiting in huts
And expecting me hourly. But even at this point
I see we are not the whole story—
A fact which will be the true burden
Of what Sister Mary will tell me
With whispering fury whenever we meet.
Already I grasp how her keys and her rosary rattle,
How her black shoes click over the parquet
Between the main hall where I'm not
And the corridor's end where the milk-crates are stacked
By the hot-pipes and stinking already,
Where too I am not—not at school,
Not there with the wintering bulbs on the shelf
Or the poster of autumn
In which all the animals crowd to the roots
Of a single encompassing tree, and the vole
And the stoat and the badger are folded
As if in their separate drawers. Not there.
She will speak of my mother and father,
To whom I am lent, of my soul, of elaborate penance,
But part of the time she will look
At the street where the afternoon darkens,
The smoke going past at the rooftops,
The sky which has cleared to an arctic blue glamour
Behind which the stars have been steadily blazing.
Lorries and funerals pass at the junction.
The canon makes calls in the parlours
Of all his insoluble Irish, his boots

Going over the leaves with a sound like salt
As the temperature drops
And the sirens of factories bray,
Plain facts of the matter
Which do not respond, being absent themselves.

NO ONE

No one, you must wait in all these rooms,
These overnight exhaustions of good humour,
In the stopped clock and the tone for *unobtainable*,
In cities we can never really see,
Where it is dark already and the windows opposite
Are this one multiplied as near
As makes no odds *ad infinitum*.

No one, you make salesmen of us all.
The hanging suits are hugged by loneliness.
The luggage has no other place to go.
The mirrors can never remember exactly
Who's who when we sit down before them
To write this in humorous terms
And invent the expenses and stare.

The rooms at our backs are the faintest idea
And you are the chill at the centre
That means we are where we belong,
Locked in, as if anything threatens
This privacy gripped like the photos
Of people we claim to have loved,
Whose faces, when we study them, are yours.

SO TELL ME

So tell me, whose anxieties are these?
The naked figures flitting from the lawn
Between two eyeblinks; those who vanish
Down the sweating aisles of the conservatory;
Who leave the pond to sway beneath its leaves,
Its steps unmarked although a print was made.

It is for them you wake at four o'clock
When light that is not light has settled
Momentarily within the garden walls,
A specious glaze on rose-leaves and black water.
It is for them that you impersonally ache,
For those unmet, who'll never hear your name

And would not care if you should see them fucking,
Bold as brass, as if they owned the place.
It is for them you peer into the pool,
Wipe back the leaves again and search
With desperation matching disbelief
For something else beside your sweating face.

VALENTINE

The other life, the properly narrated one
You glimpse through flying carriages
Is there, on the opposite platform.
A girl with a shoulderbag, reading the paper.
Frame by frame you see her,
Not her face exactly or her clothes,
But how she's self-possessed, as though
She's never heard of the alternative,
Placing, you suppose, her toe against her heel
And balancing, as though alone.
Be silent, you think, to the oaf on the public address,
The school party, the earnest Americans.
Silence, you think, to the clock flipping over its cards
Like an unemployed gambler.
Either side the railway runs away
Through cuttings, other cities, bits of scrub, past standing pools
And brickworks, birchwoods, nightfall
When the strangers' faces watch themselves,
To oceans, deserts, icecaps,
All the life you will not stake a claim to now.
But while she's there it lives,
At Doncaster and Newcastle and York,
And all through-stations of romance,
There beside the footbridge,
Auburn, dark or sooty blonde,
In velvet, in a biker jacket or in decorator's overalls,
Unbothered, never late, on all the platforms
For a lifetime, practising her liberty
Without a name, a face, a destination.

RAILWAY SONGS

Trains go past. Their effigies do likewise,
Upstairs on the layout, all afternoon.
The world is private. This is the meaning of weather—
The icicle losing its grip at the roof's edge,
The white afternoons at the far end of summer—
Weather, and trains, with the world indoors,
Advancing its strangeness over the lino.

Squint through your specs, through the fog,
Through the downpour, the clear-eyed dawn of October,
At actual engines departing the city,
Intent on the serious north. No flock-grass
Or papier mâché, tunnel, viaduct
Or working prewar German water-mill
Can take you there, yet you believe
In the place where the points are iced over
And wolves have got into the signal-box,
Leaving their pawprints across the slick parquet
And windows steamed over with signalmen's terror.

Delight, as you crouch by the paraffin heater
And idly unravel your cable-stitch pullover.
Oh to be Scotland By Rail, a grey rock
In the shape of a tender, displayed
By a smoke-coloured sea; to have become
The merest fire-blanket in the corridor
When everything falls silent, when the smoke
Has borne itself away above the snowy cutting
With a tunnel at both ends, between
The lapse of conversation and the panic.

*

Rain is vanishing the hills.
All down the line the stations go missing—
Bridges, Markets, Highest Points and Heritage
Undone by rain, the coal-fired weather
Of almost-irreparable newsreel. Whole counties

Turn to smoking stacks of viaducts
From under which, by documentary miracle,
Engines by the dozen steam
In parallel straight at us.

*

Here inside this grey-green afternoon
Is where I've always lived. It stretches
From the War until they burn me like a sleeper.

I've stayed on at home. Our railings were stolen
For weapons, they told us, which left low walls
To run like blacked-out carriages

Around the parks and cemeteries.
I'm waiting today in the shelter
While a half-mad gardener explains

How corpses drive his floral clock,
Whose movement is based upon Kilmarnock station.
At the church after service are middle-aged ladies

Who dance through the trees to a small guitar.
But the children are looking at something quite different,
The tracks, perhaps, beyond the hedge,

And the phone in the vestry keeps ringing the once
For the vicar is also this small station's master
And Bradshaw is still in his heaven.

*

When the County Grounds are hailed-on and empty
And the miserable old parties who snapped
In Leeds and Sheffield, Middlesbrough and Hull,
'We'll have that wireless off' are dead and stuffed,
The special lines remain between the cricket and their graves.

Likewise 'The masters who taught us are dead',
But we have hung on with our oddments of habit,
Pausing perhaps when the sun strikes the red and green glass
In the porch, or inclined to believe
That the groundsman was made an exception to death

And sits there grinning silently
At *Workers' Playtime* on the wireless in his hut,
With a goods train sliding past just out of earshot.

The Mallard comes steaming out of its frame
And the four-minute mile waits like Everest—
Cinder tracks everywhere, sodden and virtuous,

Coal-coloured sandshoes and wet, gritty legs,
While shunters go by, bringing rain to Hull Fair,
To the trains made of china, the trains full of goldfish,

The half-naked girl-in-a-tank-with-a-train,
The dripping back flap of the Ghost Train,
The driver's mate waving at no one.

A PROVINCIAL STATION

The brutalized youth has returned
With the compasses, sketchbook, unhealthy ideas,
From his motherless home or the military school,
To stand on the clinker beside the low shed
At one end or the other of summer.
Grey, thundery weather, the sighing of reeds.

Three days ago he left
This very place, it seems—
Birchwood, marshes, village out of sight.
The train's lugubrious siren pulls away.
Here's Kostya!
Or whatever the hell he's called,
In his all-weather coat made of sacking,
Sitting in a coma in the trap,
With the old horse, Misha,
Dead for years, tormented by mosquitoes.

THE MIDDLE

That's him finished, halfway down the hall,
His good line gone, his afterlife unsure.
Then this one's written on the mirror
With her lipstick, *Fuck you Jim.* She sits
Imprisoned in the gesture, and her breath
Will neither clear nor wholly cloud the glass
In which we glimpse ourselves behind her, there
To sympathize or think of something else.
Useless at this point to rifle the drawers
Or go over and peer through the blinds:
The hat suspended from its chute of smoke
Is there, or not. It makes no difference.
This is the case for everything in sight—
The barbershop, the take-away, the steps
That climb to the cathedral where they met;
Or down the other way towards the bridge
Where the receding globes of milky light
Have met the dark's advancing rain halfway
And are reflected far below, in what
We shall imagine is the rising tide.
We must accept the sickle moon as well,
Quite openly reclining on its page
Of rotten weather, granting with its gaze
The general irony designed for nights
That will not be remembered when at last
The horsemen choose to come, delivering
Their fire and sword, supposing that's the case.

A SECRET

There isn't much in this town to compare
With breaking into vestibules at night—
The scuffed brown panels, parquet floors,
The counter-bell you fix to make
A farting noise resembling a bluefly
Drowning in a thimble, right?
I choose the office, check the desk. The drawers
Are stuffed with ancient phone directories.
There's Lana Turner's photo on the wall,
In '49 about to shoot or sing.
She looks as if she knows what I'm about
But never tells. I sit there by the hour,
Smoking, saying, randomly, the names
Of Ma Bell's Fifties clients, wondering
What they did to get themselves in print—
I speak of you, Marzial Unzurrunzaga,
Sadie VanDerBo and Henry Polk.
I watch the hatstand's shadow on the glass
In the continued absence of the hat
Which in another story, worn by someone else
Would glide like paranoia down the hall,
Its mind on intervention, meaning facts:
I watch the sweep-hand wiping out the night
As radar would the after-hours sea,
And this ends where it started—gloves on,
Honour satisfied, my kind of justice done
And no one wiser, least of all myself.
At dawn I take the service lift back down
To walk the not-unreasonable streets. Perhaps
You wonder where the money is, the sex,
The crazed abuse of power at the top,
The screaming statues plunging to the bed.
Not me. I live the Big Beguine
And pray no explanation makes it stop.

LE VOYAGE

after Baudelaire

The child in love with maps and lithographs
Finds everywhere a match for appetite;
But though it's infinite beneath the lamp,
As memory the world sails out of sight.

One morning we embark. The mind ablaze,
The heart blown up with rancour and disease,
We set out with the rhythm of the tide,
Infinitude adrift on finite seas.

Some do it to escape the hated State;
Some flee the horrors of indoors, and some—
Stargazers blinded by a woman's stare—
Outrun the lure of Circean perfume,

And rather than be beasts consign themselves
To space and light and skies of molten brass,
Where biting cold and heat that roasts them black
Will slowly mask the imprint of her kiss.

But the authentic travellers are those
Who, light as balloons, take off and never give
Consideration to the claims of fate
And, never asking why, demand to live.

Such men's desires map themselves in clouds.
They dream, the way a squaddie dreams a gun,
Of unknown pleasures, protean and vast,
Out where the writ of language cannot run.

PAYSAGE

(a long way) after Baudelaire

To get these eclogues written I must sleep
Like an astrologer, beside the sky,
Among the belfries, hearing while I dream
The high wind bear their solemn songs away.
Chin in hand, in the remotest attic
Let me know the factories' song and blether,
Cowls and campaniles like steamer funnels,
Big skies which must also sleep forever.

The fog burns off: I see the birth of stars
Out in the blue as evening's lamps come on,
The coal-smoke glide like rivers into heaven,
The moon pour her intoxications down.
I'll dream on with my windows open wide
Until in winter's frozen monochrome
I close the shutters, lock myself away
And name the only world where I'm at home.

In the absence of horizons waits the garden:
Statues in the fountains weep and kiss,
The birds will name themselves at dawn and dusk.
Our life is nowhere much compared with this
Formality that does not need or think,
And is the whole of what can be expressed,
This graveyard on the blessed Isle of Ink
Where language learns to lay itself to rest.

HOMEWORK

That girl isn't doing her homework.
She sits in her room and looks out
At the place she grew up in.

It's neither one thing nor the other.
She looks at her parents, knee-deep
In the garden, pretending

They live somewhere else, in a dream
Of unceasing improvements.
It's summer, or nearly.

A southbound express hammers under the bridge
Past the field where the scrap-dealer's horse
Stands chained to a sleeper—

Gone in a moment
The long-shadowed field
Bitten down to the quick

With its ragged-arsed horse,
The hawthorns obscuring the buildings.
Then the next bridge and the long braking curve

To the city. The girl tilts her head
For a minute, listening
As the air re-seals itself.

'The summer trains run on all night,
Coming from northward, in blue never-darkness,
Past islands of fog, by the seashore,

Rocking the guard with his crossword,
The drunks and the children sleeping at last
When the sound of the train is like silence.'

BIOGRAPHER

Now it's time to pull yourself together.
So tip me a metaphorical wink,
There in that photograph's black-and-white weather,
Held between youth and the long dry wank
The book club wants to bind in pseudo-leather.
That's you done. I'm pouring us a drink.

Look where your imperfect tenses led.
Observe your weird insistence on the right
To live (*or else near offer*, you'd have said)
Ten thousand times the same provincial night
With third-string fucks across a narrow bed.
All here, dear heart. You shrink to fit my sights:

From birth to fluky first to shrivelled prick,
Plus cancer to confirm you're one of us.
But it's adultery that does the trick
(You *rode in style* although you *missed the bus*).
The punters need the poets to be sick:
It makes the absent gift less onerous.

Stiff with insights life could never give you,
I write what you could only wish you'd said.
Balls, of course, but who will quite believe you?
After all, I raised you from the dead.
I made you up, because I mean to live you.
Bet you wish you'd thought of me instead.

SOMETHING TO READ ON THE TRAIN

'the unknown unwanted life'—Randall Jarrell

When the lights fail at a tunnel's mouth
There is a moment when the rain's
Projected on the page and then runs dry

Across the reader's hands—the reader
Who sees this as we do and wants
To find something behind it. The reader,

Middle-aged now and knowing in detail
What a disappointment looks like,
Glimpses the shape of a roof, a lit window,

A branch line the train never follows
Through those woods and consequences;
Marks the place, unwraps a stick of gum

(This train does not encourage smoking)
And for the umpteenth time enjoys
The drops the brakes send skating off the glass,

As a station takes shape
From an arc-light, a bench and the name
Of one place, not another. I've read this

So long I've begun to invent it.
Europe's real name is Insomnia,
Night after night going over these points

As if to be elsewhere sufficiently
Often or long could amount to belief.
Night-lit rooms beside the iron road

In other languages, I want you.
Priest with a thriller; cop with a pony book;
Bore, with your Railways of Fact;

You, yes, you, with your hand down your pants;
And the hopeless case, reading this poem: let's look.
Can you show me the map of the system, the clock

That speaks German and stands at dead centre?
Even its guardian is sneaking a read:
There's a girl in a house by the railway;

A reader at night, black rain, a compartment;
A man who can't sleep but who knows
He is dreaming and cannot wake up.

THE COMMISSION

Please write some brief amusing verses
Suitable for viewing
Late on when the punters think
They could be pissed or screwing,

Or watching *Prisoner: Cell Block H*
Or papering the ceiling.
Bear in mind these facts but keep
The poem strong on feeling.

Do beware of politics
And drugs and private parts:
The issues of the day are not
The province of the arts.

And keep the language temperate—
No tits, not even bums—
For as we speak, the advertisers
Frown and do their sums.

Plus, given that we've borrowed time
From football and the weather,
Try to find a way of bringing
These two strands together,

Preferably written
In the manner of the ads,
Incorporating *Snickers*
And a plug for *My Two Dads*.

The poem should be strong and soft,
Absorbent and discreet,
Not bag around your ankles
Or leave marks upon the sheet.

It ought to satisfy the need
For hope and consolation
And stop the bastards wondering
What's on the other station.

Apart from that, what you create's
Entirely your choice,
Though we'll have an actor read it
In a proper poet's voice.

Above all, let your work be proof
That art still has a role,
Which, after all, you must admit,
Is better than the dole.

CANTONA

One touch, then turn, then open the defence,
Then, gliding down your private corridor,
Arriving as the backs go screaming out,
You slide into slow motion as you score
Again, in the heroic present tense.
As Trevor says, that's what it's all about.

Like boxing and the blues, it's poor man's art.
It's where the millions possess a gift
As vital as it looks vicarious:
While Fergie chews and struts like Bonaparte
We see the pride of London getting stiffed,
And victory falls on the Republic, *us*.

But Eric, what about that Monsieur Hyde,
Your second half, who grows *Les Fleurs du Mal*
Who shows his studs, his fangs and his disdain,
Who gets set off, then nearly sent inside
For thumping jobsworths at the *Mondiale*?
Leave thuggery to thugs and use your brain:

Now choose the spot before the ball arrives,
Now chest it, tee it, volley from the D.
Now Wimbledon, like extras, simply look,
And even Hansen feels he must agree:
This 'luxury' is why the game survives,
This poetry that steps outside the book.

PARADISE

for Harry Novak

You say that you are poor but you are happy
In this city in the north. You say
The long ceramic tunnel underneath the railway
Where you wash in what drips down
Could be the lavatory of paradise.
It has the scope, the echo and the sense
That nothing changes, ever. Anyway,
A place to winter. Lying
In the workmen's trench among the cones
In the indigent glamour of dawn
When its blue O calls at either end,
You are shat on by dogs and arrested.
You say it's the real thing at last.
Your publisher works from a concrete emplacement
Attached to a school, now defunct,
For the training of criminals and/or
Security men. He likes a place with atmosphere.
He is your friend. He will wave,
Stepping over the trench, and will sometimes remark
That he read of your case in the papers.
You think he's becoming a god:
His compound has a special right to rain
And blinding grit, through which
You can manage a harrowing glimpse
Of the metro bridge crossing the river,
Symbolic of time, and the water itself
Far below, leaving town in a hurry. As ever
You think of yourself with your overcoat
Spread like a ray, going with it, face down.
All this and the doors have no handles.
There he is, shading his eyes
From the glare of the stockroom
In which your life's work has been waiting
For this, to be burned for insurance.
It's real, you insist, as you crouch
At the letterbox, hearing the daisy-wheel
Hammer out money for someone.
You've made your trench. Now lie in it.
I am the upshot, you shout at the bridges.

The bridges shout back in Chinese.
They have not understood. You're standing
Knee-deep in the prawn-scented Ouseburn,
Attempting once more to persuade
Your gaberdine to float. Or you are rustling
At the city farm. You sit on the metro,
A sheep on each arm, and await the inspectors.
You say, when I hear the word
Culture, I reach for my arse
With both hands. Then I kiss it goodbye.

ON NOT BEING PAUL DURCAN

Let me be the first to admit it:
I am not Paul Durcan. Neither am I
Captain Bligh or Mandevil of the famous Travels
Or Prince or for that matter Debra Winger. But that is by the way.
Especially I am not Paul Durcan.
My life is more blandly confined
To the plane of the rational, to means and their ends,
Such as getting yer man to the mike
To deliver the business, ensuring the books
(*A Snail In my Prime: New and Selected Poems*)
Have arrived and the waterjug's placed
On the pure golden mean of the lectern
Or modest deal table, whichever's required
(A memo: examine the contract.) An audience, too.
Let's not forget them,
The 'A' level students brought down
In a haze of Coles' Notes off the Pennines in buses;
The poised aficionados of the art who come in late;
A scatter of lunatics haunting the fringes; and someone
Who thinks it's the Chilean evening. Hello there, Keith.
It is not my lot to expatiate grandly.
Yer man's the one gifted that way
With the left-handed head. My portion
Is booking his room at the Jackass Hotel near the station
In spite of the idiot trainee
Who answers the phone submarinely—
First language quite clearly not English
And possibly not of this planet. I do this
For love of the art of Paul Durcan.
Likewise I perform the grim divination
Of train-times as if they were true
In order that Durcan shall come to the mike
In the peak of condition and go through his paces,
That blend of exaltation and terror
For which he is everywhere famous
Except up on Tyneside, which takes it or leaves it,
Supposing it's not Basil Bunting that's on. But let's not
Get into aesthetics before they have opened the bar.

43

Give us yer suit, I have heard someone whisper
At dapper Glyn Maxwell. I hope
We shall have none of that when yer man
Steps up in his elegant corduroy leisure equipment. . . .

NEVER CAN SAY GOODBYE

(with apologies to Gloria Gaynor)

1

Farewell to Ironopolis
And both the Hartlepoolii
And windy Ashington which is
More ultima than Thule.

Farewell O Bowes Museum
Where Woolworths meets Versailles,
And Barrow of the dank hotels
Where poets go to die,

And O farewell the nuclear coast
Whose rain resembles rain:
Spectacular diseases
Are flagging down the train.

Farewell secret Bellingham,
The capital of nowhere—
Nowhere, since it never seems
Quite possible to go there.

Adieu to cloud-capped Alston,
You boreal Andorra,
To Consett where the air is crisp
And nights are like Gomorrah.

Fair Sunderland! Your gothic
Chasm has the Wear in,
Deep enough to urinate
A conurbation's beer in.

Washington, where folks get lost
And are not even pissed!
It's taken me this long to grasp
That you do not exist.

(I shouldn't mock, since where I live
Is bookless Forest Hall,
And there, as many have remarked,
No bugger lives at all.)

Since Gateshead leaves me speechless
With its Leningradic scale,
Let's linger in the Coffin Bar
And move beyond the pale . . .

2

. . . Farewell 'the flat ephemeral pamphlet',
Farewell 'the boring meeting'.
Farewell O failed grant-applicant
Who takes the yearly beating.

'This year poems have appeared
In *Sphinctre* and in *Bowel*.'
Quite so, but still the time has come
For throwing back the towel—

Mine, of course, not yours:
You'll send ad infinitum
Truckloads of your latest works.
I wonder why you write 'em—

Because you write but never read,
Because you never listen,
Because you are the porcelain
The caught-short Muses piss in?

Perhaps you wrap your brain in foil
And slam it in the oven?
Is God the source of your ideas,
Or shag-ins down the coven?

You know how you forget to spell
And punctuate and think?
Your gin-soliloquies attest
The perils of strong drink.

Love is fleeting, death is sad,
The world's a vale of pain.
In case we had forgotten this
Your poems speak it plain—

A chimpanzee could understand
The point those verses make,
And chimps I know could write it down
In half the time you take . . .

3
. . . But in the sticky-pawed abyss,
Far in the sweating night,
It strikes me like a rubber brick:
You're absolutely right:

We're meant to be Victorian
With Sentiments to match,
Be patriots more frumious
Than the fabled bandersnatch,

With language from an uncut page,
All vales and leas and wherefore,
And fairies dancing in a ring—
It's what the inkwell's there for.

We ought to write as if we died
In 1897—
Lord Bumcrack's torpid ministry,
The Queen annexing heaven,

Where ships of line still dream of sail
And foreign races blench
To face a steely British square
And no one minds the stench—

Forget the legless veteran,
A beggar on his trolley.
Clear the streets: dispose of him
With a Vickers-Armstrong volley . . .

Funny how all innocence
Leads back to politics—
Of all the stuff that time creates,
The only sort that sticks . . .

. . . I see you now, my double,
(*Mon semblable, mon frère*).
I promise I'll stay over here
If you'll stay over there:

Safe in your afterlife of Love,
Of England, Home and Duty,
Truth is in the treasury
And so, it seems, is Beauty—

Emblems on the looted urn
The Governor taps his ash in,
Far too valuable, of course,
To put the nation's cash in,

Which, coming swiftly up to date
Is why this *Page* is over.
Farewell. Weep not. Its death shall leave
Consultancies in clover.

THE PAUSE

a homeopathic poem

Across the desert of the desk
The pause extends, extends.
The clock-hands crawl discreetly. Cups
Accumulate and cool. The bin
Is full of chewing-gum. The mail
Is read, discarded, and the low sun
Fades across the city. Days of this,
Then weeks, and still the pause extends
Its anomie through every book
And synapse, memory and act.
The pen forgets its function, ink
Absents itself from inkiness, and soon
It will have been this way forever:
You were born to idleness, the world
To mindless self-regard. Therefore
I take it you were only joking when
You swore you'd packed in smoking, then.

49

READING STEVENS IN THE BATH

It is Newcastle at evening. It is far
From the furnished banks of the coaly Tyne
But close beside the hidden and infernal banks

Of the unutterable Ouseburn. Howay. It cries
Its native cry, this poisoned soup of prawns.
Howay. The evil river sings. The mind,

In Forest Hall, the haunted disbelieving suburb
Like a field of snowmen, the mind in Forest Hall
Lays by its knitting and considers

Going to the Fusilier. Howay. But in the upper room,
The room upstairs, the upstairs room,
The blear of glass and heat wherein

Not much is visible, a large pink man
Is reading Stevens in the bath. Howay. It is bath-time,
The time of the bath, the green-watered, where the mind

Lies unencumbered by the body as by time.
It is the bath as absolute, admitting
No conditional of green, the bath in which the bather

Lies considering. And the mind takes out
Its lightness to inspect, and finding nothing there
Begins to sing, embodying, emboldening its note.

It is the singing body in the bath, the mind.
Bookless Fruiterers, tell me if you can
What he may find to sing about, that man

Half-audible, and howling, as it were, the moon
That rests its gravity on weary Forest Hall,
That sends its tidal song by Tyne,

By Ouseburn, by the purifying plant
And ultimately here, to this balneum absolute,
Steam-punkah'd bath at the end of the mind, whose singer

Sings beyond the scope of tongues and sanity
Of neighbours, howling like a wolf among the snowmen
To the moon which does not listen:

Say it's only a paper moon,
Sailing over a cardboard sea,
But it wouldn't be make-believe

If you believed in me.
Howay. Howay. Howay!

AMOURS DE GRIMSBY

When the sway of the exotic overwhelmed
My lyric impulse, I returned
At length to indigence and Grimsby.
On the quay where the fish-train set me down
And pulled away for Trebizond and Cleethorpes
No gift-box of herrings awaited me this time.
After the exhaustion of my early promise
In mannered elaboration of the same few
Arid tropes, I did not find in Grimsby
Girls in states of half-undress awaiting me
When they had got their shopping from the Co-op,
Had their hair done, phoned their sisters,
Read a magazine and thought I was the one.
I was *homo Grimsby*, brought to bed on spec.
When one bar in Grimsby turned into another—
Shelf of scratchings, half-averted clock,
The glassy roar when time was done
And steam rose from the massive sinks
In which the stars of Grimsby might have bathed—
I got my amicable end away
In Grimsby, or I sat on their settees,
My arms outstretched to mothers winding wool.
Therefore I live in Grimsby, cradled
In a fishwife's scarlet arms from dusk
To hobnailed dawn, my tongue awash
With anchovies and Grimsby's bitter Brown.
Mighty Humber's middle passage shrinks
To flooded footprints on a sandbar, each in turn
Inspected by a half-attentive moon. We sit
In smoke-rooms looking out. We know
That Grimsby is the midst of life, the long
Just-opened hour with its cellophane removed,
The modest editorial in which the world
Might change but does not, when the cellars
Empty back their waters, when the tide that comes
Discreetly to the doors enquires for old sake's sake
If this could be the night to sail away. From Grimsby?

R = U = B = R = I = C

It will not feature streetlamps, gable-ends
Or someone's fence thrown down by recent gales.
It will not tell us in a sidelong way
About your family's escape from Europe
In a *wagon-lit* disguised as pierrots, through forests
Thick with gamekeepers-turned-Nazis. It will not
Pine for Bukovina or for Rochdale.
It will not be Eurocentric, but in general
Atlases will leave it quite unmoved.
It will not satirize the times
Or praise a different period in terms
Which challenge our conception of the Good.
It will ignore the claims to eccentricity alleged
Among its fellow travellers on the Metro.
The library's oilclothed tables will not grant it
Access to black pools of divination.
It will not sing of ordinary life—
Of football, vinegar, domestic violence—
Or stake the claims of art by means
Of imagery drawn from books of reproductions
Where the hero in a black suit stands
Before a maze of ice, or—donning a monastic cowl—
Among the sullen precincts of a temple
Framed with cypresses, to which a black-sailed ship
Draws near. It will not be ironic.
It will not speak to you in person
In an upper room where twelve are gathered
At the taxpayer's expense to hear
An explanation of themselves before they go
For pizza and a row. You will not hear it
Hail you in the accents of broad comedy or Ras Ta Far I
As you sit and mind your business on the bus
Or in a padded cell. You cannot make it
Speak to your condition, nor to those
With a different sexual orientation,
Nor to those who neither know nor care to know
A poem from a cabbage or *Nintendo*.
Ask it not here, it won't be saying.
It will not glozingly insinuate itself
Through broadcast media. Sunday teatime's

Safe for washing up and dismal contemplation
Of the weather which it also does not deal with.
It will not come between you and your lover
With a sudden intimation on the stairs
That all is lost, or place its hand imploringly
Upon your knee. It does not want to sleep with you,
Still less to drink its Vimto from your slipper;
Could not give a flying fuck for Nature
In its purest form or when as reconceived
At court it turns to pastoral; while God
Has never captured its attention fully—
Likewise the plains of Hell, the void or any
Combination of the three. It will not bear
The mark of Satan or the Library of Congress.
It will not write abuse in lipstick
On the mirror. Neither will it urinate
Upon the carpet having nicked the video.
It leaves the bathroom as we found it, like the world.
It would not slide the bad news from its folder,
Come to pray with you or hold your hand
As you confess a life of misdemeanours.
Nor will it permit you to interpret
Any of its absent gestures so
As to suggest an ur-, a sub-, a meta-text,
Having neither faith nor doubt
Nor any inclination worth a name, except
To know that it's what neither you nor I
Nor any of the pronouns lives to write,
Although we serve its sentence. Now begin.

OXFORD POETS

Fleur Adcock
Moniza Alvi
Kamau Brathwaite
Joseph Brodsky
Basil Bunting
Daniela Crăsnaru
Michael Donaghy
Keith Douglas
D. J. Enright
Roy Fisher
Ida Affleck Graves
Ivor Gurney
David Harsent
Gwen Harwood
Anthony Hecht
Zbigniew Herbert
Thomas Kinsella
Brad Leithauser
Derek Mahon
Jamie McKendrick

Sean O'Brien
Peter Porter
Craig Raine
Zsuzsa Rakovszky
Henry Reed
Christopher Reid
Stephen Romer
Carole Satyamurti
Peter Scupham
Jo Shapcott
Penelope Shuttle
Anne Stevenson
George Szirtes
Grete Tartler
Edward Thomas
Charles Tomlinson
Marina Tsvetaeva
Chris Wallace-Crabbe
Hugo Williams